I0621993

Meditating on the Joyful Mysteries

An Intentional Rosary

Amy Schisler

Bozman, MD 2023

ISBN: 979-8-9883677-5-8

Published by:
Chesapeake Sunrise Publishing
Amy Schisler
Bozman, MD
2023

$\mathcal{T}$able of Contents

For the grace of Hope:
Hail Mary, full of grace.
The Lord is with thee.
Blessed art thou among women,
And blessed is the fruit of thy womb,
Jesus.
Holy Mary, Mother of God,
Pray for us sinners,
Now and at the hour of death.
Amen

For the grace of Charity:
Hail Mary, full of grace.
The Lord is with thee.
Blessed art thou among women,
And blessed is the fruit of thy womb,
Jesus.
Holy Mary, Mother of God,
Pray for us sinners,
Now and at the hour of death.
Amen

Glory be to the Father,
And the Son,
And the Holy Spirit,
As now and ever shall be,
World without end.
Amen

*T*he First Luminous Mystery:

The Baptism of Christ in the Jordan

Matthew 3:13-17

Then Jesus came from Galilee to John at the Jordan to be baptized by him. John tried to prevent him, saying, "I need to be baptized by you, and yet you are coming to me?"

Jesus said to him in reply, "Allow it now, for thus it is fitting for us to fulfill all righteousness." Then he allowed him.

After Jesus was baptized, he came up from the water and behold, the heavens were opened [for him], and he saw the Spirit of God descending like a dove [and] coming upon him. And a voice came from the heavens, saying, "This is my beloved Son, with whom I am well pleased."

Our Father, who art in Heaven, hallowed be thy name.
Thy kingdom come.
Thy will be done on Earth as it is in

Heaven.

Give us this day our daily bread,
And forgive us our trespasses as we
forgive those who trespass against us.
And lead us not into temptation, but
deliver us from evil.
Amen

*For all those being baptized into the family of
Christ:*
Hail Mary, full of grace.
The Lord is with thee.
Blessed art thou among women,
And blessed is the fruit of thy womb,
Jesus.
Holy Mary, Mother of God,
Pray for us sinners,
Now and at the hour of death.
Amen

*For all Godparents, especially new ones, that
they always live according to their promise to
their Godchildren:*
Hail Mary, full of grace.
The Lord is with thee.
Blessed art thou among women,
And blessed is the fruit of thy womb,

Jesus.
Holy Mary, Mother of God,
Pray for us sinners,
Now and at the hour of death.
Amen

For those who have not been baptized:
Hail Mary, full of grace.
The Lord is with thee.
Blessed art thou among women,
And blessed is the fruit of thy womb,
Jesus.
Holy Mary, Mother of God,
Pray for us sinners,
Now and at the hour of death.
Amen

*For those baptized who have forgotten that they
belong to God and His Church:*
Hail Mary, full of grace.
The Lord is with thee.
Blessed art thou among women,
And blessed is the fruit of thy womb,
Jesus.
Holy Mary, Mother of God,
Pray for us sinners,

Now and at the hour of death.
Amen

For all new Catholics just entering the Church:
Hail Mary, full of grace.
The Lord is with thee.
Blessed art thou among women,
And blessed is the fruit of thy womb,
Jesus.
Holy Mary, Mother of God,
Pray for us sinners,
Now and at the hour of death.
Amen

For a deep, conscious renewal of our baptismal vows:
Hail Mary, full of grace.
The Lord is with thee.
Blessed art thou among women,
And blessed is the fruit of thy womb,
Jesus.
Holy Mary, Mother of God,
Pray for us sinners,
Now and at the hour of death.
Amen

For bishops, priests, deacons, and all who

baptize the faithful:
Hail Mary, full of grace.
The Lord is with thee.
Blessed art thou among women,
And blessed is the fruit of thy womb,
Jesus.
Holy Mary, Mother of God,
Pray for us sinners,
Now and at the hour of death.
Amen

For all those who have taken vows of religious orders:
Hail Mary, full of grace.
The Lord is with thee.
Blessed art thou among women,
And blessed is the fruit of thy womb,
Jesus.
Holy Mary, Mother of God,
Pray for us sinners,
Now and at the hour of death.
Amen

For those waiting for and praying to hear the voice of God in their lives:
Hail Mary, full of grace.
The Lord is with thee.

Blessed art thou among women,
And blessed is the fruit of thy womb,
Jesus.
Holy Mary, Mother of God,
Pray for us sinners,
Now and at the hour of death.
Amen

*That our actions will be pleasing to God and
His Son:*
Hail Mary, full of grace.
The Lord is with thee.
Blessed art thou among women,
And blessed is the fruit of thy womb,
Jesus.
Holy Mary, Mother of God,
Pray for us sinners,
Now and at the hour of death.
Amen

Glory be to the Father,
And the Son,
And the Holy Spirit,
As now and ever shall be,
World without end.
Amen

O my Jesus, forgive us our sins, save us from the fires of hell; lead all souls to Heaven, especially those who have most need of your mercy.

*T*he Second Luminous Mystery:
The Wedding Feast at Cana
John 2:1-11

On the third day there was a wedding in Cana in Galilee, and the mother of Jesus was there. Jesus and his disciples were also invited to the wedding.

When the wine ran short, the mother of Jesus said to him, "They have no wine." [And] Jesus said to her, "Woman, how does your concern affect me? My hour has not yet come." His mother said to the servers, "Do whatever he tells you."

Now there were six stone water jars there for Jewish ceremonial washings, each holding twenty to thirty gallons. Jesus told them, "Fill the jars with water." So they filled them to the brim. Then he told them, "Draw some out now and take it to the headwaiter." So they took it. And when the headwaiter tasted the water that had become wine, without knowing where it came from (although the servers who had drawn the water knew), the headwaiter called the

*bridegroom and said to him, "Everyone serves
good wine first, and then when people have
drunk freely, an inferior one; but you have kept
the good wine until now."*

*Jesus did this as the beginning of his signs in
Cana in Galilee and so revealed his glory, and
his disciples began to believe in him.*

Our Father, who art in Heaven, hallowed
be thy name.
Thy kingdom come.
Thy will be done on Earth as it is in
Heaven.
Give us this day our daily bread,
And forgive us our trespasses as we
forgive those who trespass against us.
And lead us not into temptation, but
deliver us from evil.
Amen

For all married couples:
Hail Mary, full of grace.
The Lord is with thee.
Blessed art thou among women,
And blessed is the fruit of thy womb,

Jesus.
Holy Mary, Mother of God,
Pray for us sinners,
Now and at the hour of death.
Amen

For all couples preparing for the Sacrament of Marriage:
Hail Mary, full of grace.
The Lord is with thee.
Blessed art thou among women,
And blessed is the fruit of thy womb,
Jesus.
Holy Mary, Mother of God,
Pray for us sinners,
Now and at the hour of death.
Amen

For bishops, priests, and deacons who perform the Sacrament of Marriage:
Hail Mary, full of grace.
The Lord is with thee.
Blessed art thou among women,
And blessed is the fruit of thy womb,
Jesus.
Holy Mary, Mother of God,
Pray for us sinners,

Now and at the hour of death.
Amen

For parents of brides and grooms planning upcoming weddings:
Hail Mary, full of grace.
The Lord is with thee.
Blessed art thou among women,
And blessed is the fruit of thy womb, Jesus.
Holy Mary, Mother of God,
Pray for us sinners,
Now and at the hour of death.
Amen

For all those who rejoice with newly married couples:
Hail Mary, full of grace.
The Lord is with thee.
Blessed art thou among women,
And blessed is the fruit of thy womb, Jesus.
Holy Mary, Mother of God,
Pray for us sinners,
Now and at the hour of death.
Amen

For troubled marriages:
Hail Mary, full of grace.
The Lord is with thee.
Blessed art thou among women,
And blessed is the fruit of thy womb,
Jesus.
Holy Mary, Mother of God,
Pray for us sinners,
Now and at the hour of death.
Amen

*That the wine growers in the Kingdom of God
will yield a fruitful harvest of believers:*
Hail Mary, full of grace.
The Lord is with thee.
Blessed art thou among women,
And blessed is the fruit of thy womb,
Jesus.
Holy Mary, Mother of God,
Pray for us sinners,
Now and at the hour of death.
Amen

*That all mothers will guide their children toward
God and His Church:*
Hail Mary, full of grace.
The Lord is with thee.

Blessed art thou among women,
And blessed is the fruit of thy womb,
Jesus.
Holy Mary, Mother of God,
Pray for us sinners,
Now and at the hour of death.
Amen

That we all will be filled with the grace and fruits of the Holy Spirit:
Hail Mary, full of grace.
The Lord is with thee.
Blessed art thou among women,
And blessed is the fruit of thy womb,
Jesus.
Holy Mary, Mother of God,
Pray for us sinners,
Now and at the hour of death.
Amen

That Jesus's glory will be revealed to all who believe:
Hail Mary, full of grace.
The Lord is with thee.
Blessed art thou among women,
And blessed is the fruit of thy womb,

Jesus.
Holy Mary, Mother of God,
Pray for us sinners,
Now and at the hour of death.
Amen

Glory be to the Father,
And the Son,
And the Holy Spirit,
As now and ever shall be,
World without end.
Amen

O my Jesus, forgive us our sins, save us
from the fires of hell; lead all souls to
Heaven, especially those who have most
need of your mercy.

*T*he Third Luminous Mystery:

The Proclamation of the Coming of the Kingdom of God

Mark 1:14-15; Luke 4:16-21

After John had been arrested, Jesus came to Galilee proclaiming the gospel of God:

"This is the time of fulfillment. The kingdom of God is at hand. Repent, and believe in the gospel."

He stood up to read and was handed a scroll of the prophet Isaiah. He unrolled the scroll and found the passage where it was written:

"The Spirit of the Lord is upon me, because he has anointed me to bring glad tidings to the poor. He has sent me to proclaim liberty to captives and recovery of sight to the blind, to let the oppressed go free, and to proclaim a year acceptable to the Lord."

Rolling up the scroll, he handed it back to the attendant and sat down, and the eyes of all in the synagogue looked intently at him. He said to them, "Today this scripture passage is fulfilled in your hearing."

Our Father, who art in Heaven, hallowed be thy name.
Thy kingdom come.
Thy will be done on Earth as it is in Heaven.
Give us this day our daily bread,
And forgive us our trespasses as we forgive those who trespass against us.
And lead us not into temptation, but deliver us from evil.
Amen

That all people will accept God's call to repentance:
Hail Mary, full of grace.
The Lord is with thee.
Blessed art thou among women,
And blessed is the fruit of thy womb, Jesus.
Holy Mary, Mother of God,
Pray for us sinners,
Now and at the hour of death.
Amen

That everyone will come to believe in the Gospel of the Lord:
Hail Mary, full of grace.
The Lord is with thee.
Blessed art thou among women,
And blessed is the fruit of thy womb, Jesus.
Holy Mary, Mother of God,
Pray for us sinners,
Now and at the hour of death.
Amen

In thanksgiving for the grace and mercy of our Lord, Jesus Christ:
Hail Mary, full of grace.
The Lord is with thee.
Blessed art thou among women,
And blessed is the fruit of thy womb, Jesus.
Holy Mary, Mother of God,
Pray for us sinners,
Now and at the hour of death.
Amen

For all those who rightly proclaim the Kingdom

of God:
Hail Mary, full of grace.
The Lord is with thee.
Blessed art thou among women,
And blessed is the fruit of thy womb,
Jesus.
Holy Mary, Mother of God,
Pray for us sinners,
Now and at the hour of death.
Amen

*That we will be made aware of how to proclaim
the Kingdom of God in our lives:*
Hail Mary, full of grace.
The Lord is with thee.
Blessed art thou among women,
And blessed is the fruit of thy womb,
Jesus.
Holy Mary, Mother of God,
Pray for us sinners,
Now and at the hour of death.
Amen

*That the Spirit of the Lord will be on each of us
to guide us to eternity:*
Hail Mary, full of grace.
The Lord is with thee.

Blessed art thou among women,
And blessed is the fruit of thy womb,
Jesus.
Holy Mary, Mother of God,
Pray for us sinners,
Now and at the hour of death.
Amen

*That we can live in a world where there are glad
tidings for the poor, liberty to captives, sight for
the blind, and freedom for the oppressed:*
Hail Mary, full of grace.
The Lord is with thee.
Blessed art thou among women,
And blessed is the fruit of thy womb,
Jesus.
Holy Mary, Mother of God,
Pray for us sinners,
Now and at the hour of death.
Amen

That our lives may be acceptable to the Lord:
Hail Mary, full of grace.
The Lord is with thee.
Blessed art thou among women,
And blessed is the fruit of thy womb,

Blessed art thou among women,
And blessed is the fruit of thy womb,
Jesus.
Holy Mary, Mother of God,
Pray for us sinners,
Now and at the hour of death.
Amen

*For forgiveness for the times I have led others on
a path of destruction:*
Hail Mary, full of grace.
The Lord is with thee.
Blessed art thou among women,
And blessed is the fruit of thy womb,
Jesus.
Holy Mary, Mother of God,
Pray for us sinners,
Now and at the hour of death.
Amen

Glory be to the Father,
And the Son,
And the Holy Spirit,
As now and ever shall be,
World without end.
Amen

O my Jesus, forgive us our sins, save us from the fires of hell; lead all souls to Heaven, especially those who have most need of your mercy.

*T*he Fourth Sorrowful Mystery:
The Carrying of the Cross
John 19:14-16; Matthew 27:32-33

It was preparation day for Passover, and it was about noon. And he said to the Jews, "Behold, your king!" They cried out, "Take him away, take him away! Crucify him!" Pilate said to them, "Shall I crucify your king?" The chief priests answered, "We have no king but Caesar." Then he handed him over to them to be crucified.

As they were going out, they met a Cyrenian named Simon; this man they pressed into service to carry his cross.

And…they came to a place called Golgotha (which means Place of the Skull).

Our Father, who art in Heaven, hallowed be thy name.
Thy kingdom come.
Thy will be done on Earth as it is in Heaven.
Give us this day our daily bread,

And forgive us our trespasses as we
forgive those who trespass against us.
And lead us not into temptation, but
deliver us from evil.
Amen

*That we will always remember who our true king
is:*
Hail Mary, full of grace.
The Lord is with thee.
Blessed art thou among women,
And blessed is the fruit of thy womb,
Jesus.
Holy Mary, Mother of God,
Pray for us sinners,
Now and at the hour of death.
Amen

*For those who choose they ways of men over the
ways of God:*
Hail Mary, full of grace.
The Lord is with thee.
Blessed art thou among women,
And blessed is the fruit of thy womb,
Jesus.
Holy Mary, Mother of God,
Pray for us sinners,

Now and at the hour of death.
Amen

For those who are pressed into service to help others:
Hail Mary, full of grace.
The Lord is with thee.
Blessed art thou among women,
And blessed is the fruit of thy womb,
Jesus.
Holy Mary, Mother of God,
Pray for us sinners,
Now and at the hour of death.
Amen

For those who choose careers or vocations through which they can help others:
Hail Mary, full of grace.
The Lord is with thee.
Blessed art thou among women,
And blessed is the fruit of thy womb,
Jesus.
Holy Mary, Mother of God,
Pray for us sinners,
Now and at the hour of death.
Amen

For those who volunteer in shelters, food

pantries, soup kitchens, pregnancy centers, and all places where they help those in need:
Hail Mary, full of grace.
The Lord is with thee.
Blessed art thou among women,
And blessed is the fruit of thy womb, Jesus.
Holy Mary, Mother of God,
Pray for us sinners,
Now and at the hour of death.
Amen

For those who see the face of God in the most unexpected people and places:
Hail Mary, full of grace.
The Lord is with thee.
Blessed art thou among women,
And blessed is the fruit of thy womb, Jesus.
Holy Mary, Mother of God,
Pray for us sinners,
Now and at the hour of death.
Amen

For those who willingly accept their crosses to carry:

Hail Mary, full of grace.
The Lord is with thee.
Blessed art thou among women,
And blessed is the fruit of thy womb,
Jesus.
Holy Mary, Mother of God,
Pray for us sinners,
Now and at the hour of death.
Amen

For those who try to carry the crosses of others:
Hail Mary, full of grace.
The Lord is with thee.
Blessed art thou among women,
And blessed is the fruit of thy womb,
Jesus.
Holy Mary, Mother of God,
Pray for us sinners,
Now and at the hour of death.
Amen

*For those who are walking their final steps on
this earth:*
Hail Mary, full of grace.
The Lord is with thee.
Blessed art thou among women,
And blessed is the fruit of thy womb,

Jesus.
Holy Mary, Mother of God,
Pray for us sinners,
Now and at the hour of death.
Amen

*That those who are contemplating picking up
their crosses and following Jesus:*
Hail Mary, full of grace.
The Lord is with thee.
Blessed art thou among women,
And blessed is the fruit of thy womb,
Jesus.
Holy Mary, Mother of God,
Pray for us sinners,
Now and at the hour of death.
Amen

Glory be to the Father,
And the Son,
And the Holy Spirit,
As now and ever shall be,
World without end.
Amen

O my Jesus, forgive us our sins, save us

from the fires of hell; lead all souls to Heaven, especially those who have most need of your mercy.

*T*he Fifth Sorrowful Mystery:
The Crucifixion of Death
John 19:25; Luke 23:35-46

Standing by the cross of Jesus were his mother and his mother's sister, Mary the wife of Clopas, and Mary of Magdala.

The people stood by and watched; the rulers, meanwhile, sneered at him and said, "He saved others, let him save himself if he is the chosen one, the Messiah of God." Even the soldiers jeered at him. As they approached to offer him wine they called out, "If you are King of the Jews, save yourself." Above him there was an inscription that read, "This is the King of the Jews."

Now one of the criminals hanging there reviled Jesus, saying, "Are you not the Messiah? Save yourself and us." The other, however, rebuking him, said in reply, "Have you no fear of God, for you are subject to the same condemnation? And indeed, we have been condemned justly, for the sentence we received corresponds to our

crimes, but this man has done nothing criminal."
Then he said, "Jesus, remember me when you
come into your kingdom." He replied to him,
"Amen, I say to you, today you will be with me
in Paradise."

It was now about noon and darkness came over
the whole land until three in the afternoon
because of an eclipse of the sun. Then the veil of
the temple was torn down the middle. Jesus cried
out in a loud voice, "Father, into your hands I
commend my spirit"; and when he had said this
he breathed his last.

Our Father, who art in Heaven, hallowed
be thy name.
Thy kingdom come.
Thy will be done on Earth as it is in
Heaven.
Give us this day our daily bread,
And forgive us our trespasses as we
forgive those who trespass against us.
And lead us not into temptation, but
deliver us from evil.
Amen
For those who stand by the bedside of those who

are dying:
Hail Mary, full of grace.
The Lord is with thee.
Blessed art thou among women,
And blessed is the fruit of thy womb,
Jesus.
Holy Mary, Mother of God,
Pray for us sinners,
Now and at the hour of death.
Amen

For those who must watch their loved ones suffer:
Hail Mary, full of grace.
The Lord is with thee.
Blessed art thou among women,
And blessed is the fruit of thy womb,
Jesus.
Holy Mary, Mother of God,
Pray for us sinners,
Now and at the hour of death.
Amen

*For those who stand by and watch injustice, may
they be moved to intervene:*
Hail Mary, full of grace.
The Lord is with thee.

Blessed art thou among women,
And blessed is the fruit of thy womb,
Jesus.
Holy Mary, Mother of God,
Pray for us sinners,
Now and at the hour of death.
Amen

For those who offer no help to others, that they will see the error of their ways:
Hail Mary, full of grace.
The Lord is with thee.
Blessed art thou among women,
And blessed is the fruit of thy womb,
Jesus.
Holy Mary, Mother of God,
Pray for us sinners,
Now and at the hour of death.
Amen

For the times we have sneered at God:
Hail Mary, full of grace.
The Lord is with thee.
Blessed art thou among women,
And blessed is the fruit of thy womb,
Jesus.
Holy Mary, Mother of God,

Pray for us sinners,
Now and at the hour of death.
Amen

For all those who have rejected God's gift of salvation:
Hail Mary, full of grace.
The Lord is with thee.
Blessed art thou among women,
And blessed is the fruit of thy womb,
Jesus.
Holy Mary, Mother of God,
Pray for us sinners,
Now and at the hour of death.
Amen

For prisoners and criminals seeking repentance:
Hail Mary, full of grace.
The Lord is with thee.
Blessed art thou among women,
And blessed is the fruit of thy womb,
Jesus.
Holy Mary, Mother of God,
Pray for us sinners,
Now and at the hour of death.
Amen

For the faithful who wish to be with God in Paradise:
Hail Mary, full of grace.
The Lord is with thee.
Blessed art thou among women,
And blessed is the fruit of thy womb,
Jesus.
Holy Mary, Mother of God,
Pray for us sinners,
Now and at the hour of death.
Amen

For those people we need to forgive, including ourselves:
Hail Mary, full of grace.
The Lord is with thee.
Blessed art thou among women,
And blessed is the fruit of thy womb,
Jesus.
Holy Mary, Mother of God,
Pray for us sinners,
Now and at the hour of death.
Amen

For those who are breathing their last breath:
Hail Mary, full of grace.
The Lord is with thee.

Blessed art thou among women,
And blessed is the fruit of thy womb,
Jesus.
Holy Mary, Mother of God,
Pray for us sinners,
Now and at the hour of death.
Amen

Glory be to the Father,
And the Son,
And the Holy Spirit,
As now and ever shall be,
World without end.
Amen

O my Jesus, forgive us our sins, save us
from the fires of hell; lead all souls to
Heaven, especially those who have most
need of your mercy.

*T*he End of the Rosary

Hail, Holy Queen, Mother of Mercy,
our life, our sweetness and our hope.
To thee do we cry,
poor banished children of Eve.
To thee do we send up our sighs,
mourning and weeping in this valley of
tears.
Turn then, most gracious advocate,
thine eyes of mercy toward us,
and after this our exile
show unto us the blessed fruit of thy
womb, Jesus.
O clement, O loving,
O sweet Virgin Mary.

Pray for us, O holy Mother of God.
That we may be made worthy of the
promises of Christ

O God, whose Only Begotten Son, by
his life, Death, and Resurrection, has
purchased for us the rewards of eternal
life, grant, we beseech thee, that while
meditating on these mysteries of the

most holy Rosary of the Blessed Virgin Mary, we may imitate what they contain and obtain what they promise, through the same Christ our Lord. Amen.

*T*he Memorare

Remember, O most gracious Virgin Mary, that never was it known that anyone who fled to thy protection, implored thy help, or sought thy intercession, was left unaided.

Inspired by this confidence I fly unto thee, O Virgin of virgins, my Mother.

To thee do I come, before thee I stand, sinful and sorrowful.

O Mother of the Word Incarnate, despise not my petitions, but in thy mercy hear and answer me.

Amen.

In the Name of the Father, and of the Son, and of the Holy Spirit.

Amen

*P*rayers and Petitions